The
Thinking
Man's
Guide
To
Life

The Thinking Man's *Guide To Life*

How to network,
de-stress, make friends
and everything
in-between

Alfred Tong
Illustrated by Sarah Tanat-Jones

hardie grant books

CONTENTS

INTRODUCTION

You are holding within your hands a self-help book. There, I've said it: self-help book. Now, if you're the type of person who quietly agonises over what people might think of your carefully curated, Instagrammable bookshelf, don't worry! There's actually a long and distinguished history of books of this kind, and one to which this one is hugely indebted. For what are *The Book of the Courtier* by Castiglione and *The Art of War* by Sun Tzu, if not self-help guides for the upwardly mobile Italian aristocrat and the Zhou dynasty warlord, respectively?

Combining the latest insights from neuroscientists and psychologists alongside timeless thoughts from history's greatest philosophers, *The Thinking Man's Guide to Life* offers invaluable advice on everything from how to get a decent night's sleep to how to make friends, all in

a bitesize format. Read this book to be less stressed, more successful and, generally, a nicer sort of person. If, as Lord Chesterton once said: 'Style is the dress of thoughts,' then think of this book as the new three-piece suit of your mind.

A lot of it deals with the various travails of the internet age: namely, how we can stop our mobile phones from bothering us and setting us on edge all the time. There is, of course, a fairly simple solution: just turn the bloody things off! However, we need them to be on for work and love and all the rest of it, so it's about being a little more deliberate and strategic in how we use the internet and smartphones.

And what about when we get off our phones? No doubt we'd like to be sexier, cooler, more charming and charismatic. Any book that promises you these things in three easy steps is delusional. But the psychology and history of charm and his more boisterous cousin, charisma, are genuinely interesting. You'd be amazed by how much we're suckers for a charmer and how terrible things can get when we're overly dazzled by charisma.

Overall, this book should help you cast a more discerning and sceptical eye over the ideas and trends that supposedly constitute 'modernity', but which are, in fact, rather stupid. Like the idea that brainstorms help with creative thought, or that it's a good idea to outsource your brain to the internet. People are better than computers, and face-to-face conversations, not smart phones, are responsible for new thoughts and ideas.

'If, as Lord Chesterton once said: 'Style is the dress of thoughts,' then think of this book as the new three-piece suit of your mind.'

CHAPTER ONE

WORK

HOW TO GET EMAIL
UNDER CONTROL

According to the *Harvard Business Review*, the average worker spends up to eight hours per week on email, dipping into their inboxes an average of 74 times a day. What's more, 50 per cent of the emails managers read and respond to are irrelevant to their work.

And that's not all – according to research by King's College London, all this cc'ing is quite literally making us (more) stupid. 'We lose up to ten IQ points when we interrupt work to check email,' says Jocelyn K. Glei, author of *Unsubscribe: How to Kill Email Anxiety, Avoid Distractions, and Get Real Work Done.* 'That's more than being stoned on weed.'

'We lose up to
ten IQ points
when we
interrupt work
to check email.
That's more
than being
stoned
on weed.'

So why is it so addictive? 'Neurologically, email operates like a slot machine, or what neuroscientists call a random reward system,' says Glei. 'Most of the email you receive will be junk or a bothersome work request. But sometimes you'll get something exciting, such as a flattering invitation. It's this random reward that makes email so addictive. It activates a primal impulse in our brain to seek out reward.'

So here's how to not only cut down the amount of time we spend on email, but also become more effective at communicating via email, making us less annoying to our colleagues and business partners.

WRITE A TO-DO LIST

Funnily enough, we're at our least productive when staring at our inbox hoping for that amazing invite or job offer which never seems to arrive, no matter how many times you hit the refresh button. We are most likely to fall into the 'random reward trap' when we are feeling aimless. The way to beat it is by writing a to-do list before starting work so that we can get our dopamine hit from 'real rewards', i.e. by doing the work we care about. 'This empowers you to kick off the working day with clarity and momentum,' says Glei. 'It means you have a framework for the day's priorities in place before you check your email, allowing you to weigh any incoming requests against what you've already planned to accomplish. Be realistic as you craft your to-do list. Crossing everything off is your reward, and it will also reinforce the positive behaviour.'

USE 'COMPLETION BIAS'
TO YOUR ADVANTAGE

Two hundred emails, 150 emails, 100 emails, zero emails. Aahhhh! Ever get that 'inbox zero' feeling? Feels good, doesn't it? Until you find out you've done nothing of worth whatsoever, apart from tell Kevin in accounts that, yes, you will be coming to his leaving drinks. The compulsion to get to inbox zero is driven by what neuroscientists call 'completion bias', which gives our brains a juicy hit of dopamine. The key to using completion bias to your advantage is to visualise signs of progress in the work you care about. 'It's easy to see progress on meaningless technology-based tasks, whereas it's difficult to keep track of complex, long-term creative projects that will have the most impact on our lives,' says Glei. 'When I'm writing a book, I keep a visual record of the number of words I've written each day on a calendar. Designers could stick prototypes or drafts up on the wall.'

REPLY IN BATCHES

There are two types of emailer: reactors, who react to emails when they arrive, allowing it to nibble away at their time, and batchers, who set aside specific chunks of the day to send and respond to emails, making their time more productive. 'To get yourself into the groove of batching, I recommend setting aside two to three blocks of 30–45 minutes per day for checking email,' says Glei. For important clients or bosses who expect a faster response, Gmail and Android have VIP notification options, which will alert you when specific contacts email.

USE EMOJIS :)))

According to Daniel Goleman, author of *Emotional Intelligence* and a leading scientist in the field of emotional intelligence, there is a negativity bias to email hardwired into us at a neural level. This means that if the tone of an email is neutral, we automatically assume the tone is negative. 'This point relates particularly to men, who have a bias towards a just-the-facts approach, which they associate with efficiency,' says Goleman. 'Use positive language, express some personality and opinion to increase your chances of a response, especially when you're reaching out to someone you don't know.' Anything that helps to lighten the tone, including emoticons, is permissible :)))

MAKE IT SNAPPY

Why you? Why me? Framing any request with these two questions in mind will help you get to the nub of your email much more efficiently, while still retaining a sense of charm. 'Make sure you're being concise,' says Glei. 'Lead with the request, establish your credibility and explain why it's relevant to them.' Be sure to set up the next step clearly and set a deadline – busy people love deadlines because they allow them to prioritise.

HOW TO MAKE CONVERSATION

Walk into a modern office and you might think you've entered a morgue such is the deafening silence, which is punctuated only by the tippy tap of keyboards and mice, the odd vibration from a mobile and the muted beats from someone's headphones. Is this what our trendy open-plan collaborative workspaces were designed for? Monk-like silence?

Conversation, the most fun you can have with your clothes on, is slowly going out of fashion. According to research carried out by Ipsos Mori for Deloitte in 2016, the number of device owners in the UK who made at least one voice call a week fell from 96 per cent to 75 per cent over the previous three years.

So why talk? Catherine Blyth, a journalist and author of *The Art of Conversation*, says that with textual communication there's huge scope for misunderstanding that can easily be cleared up with face-to-face or phone conversations. 'A face-to-face conversation is a multi-channel exchange of information,' she says. 'You get the sound of their voice and the expression on their face. You'll see or hear when they're obviously embarrassed, or when they're clearly losing interest. You can make a connection; you can laugh. Get on with others and you will get on in life, and enjoy it more.' Blyth says that those who are good at talking are the ones to get dates and win contracts.'

Clearly IRL conversation has applications outside of the world of work, but it is both strange and sad that younger colleagues, especially, are often flummoxed when presented with the challenge of actually speaking to someone. But not only will having a conversation save you time, so that you can carry on Tindering and WhatsApping, but it is also fun. And how often can you say that about work?

THE PHONE IS MIGHTIER
THAN THE EMAIL

We all know that email is a brilliant way to get bodies of work from one person to the next. 'It's an excellent postal system,' says Blyth. 'But if you want to discuss something or reach a conclusion about what to do next, then why not pick up the phone?'

Here are some tips for how to have a successful phone conversation with someone you've never spoken to before:

1.	Establish the reason why you're calling before you call. And be clear about what the best way of achieving your objective is.
2.	Show your courtesy by respecting their time and ask if they're available to talk.
3.	Be clear about who you are, why you're calling and why it's beneficial to them that you talk. Once you've established the purpose of the conversation and why it's relevant to them, there will be a clear connection between you.
4.	Get them to say 'yes'. Getting someone to say 'yes' to anything automatically makes them more agreeable.
5.	Be polite and amusing, warm and interested.

LISTEN MORE, TALK LESS

The philosopher Epictetus famously said, 'We have two ears and one mouth so that we can listen twice as much as we speak.' Follow that ratio. This is as true in life as it is in having a good conversation, whether on the phone or face to face.

It's a common mistake to think of conversation as a performance. 'People mistake conversation for broadcasting, when it's more like a dance with another person,' says Blyth. 'If you put all your emotional energy and curiosity into listening to them and learning about them, you become far less self-conscious. It's about demonstrating you've attended to another human being.'

SHOW THAT YOU'RE LISTENING

Active listening is how you visually and verbally demonstrate to the other person that you're actually listening. Not only is it incredibly flattering, but it also allows you to clear up misunderstandings in real time. You can do this by summarising the points they've just made to make sure you've understood them correctly. 'Demonstrate you're listening by nodding or smiling or making affirmative noises,' says Blyth. 'Or even more useful, say, "OK, if I understand you correctly, what you're saying is …" Then you're giving them the opportunity to say, "No, that's not what I meant." Or they'll say, "Exactly." And they'll feel delighted because you've demonstrated that you've heard what they've got to say, which is what everyone wants: recognition.'

'People mistake conversation for broadcasting, when it's more like a dance with another person.'

THE POWER PAUSE

Pat Kavanagh, the literary agent who was married to Julian Barnes, wielded colossal power, even though she was quite shy. 'She knew how to wait in silence,' says Blyth. 'If a publisher rang up with an offer for a book, she would not respond. Nature abhors a vacuum. People would ramble on, and that's a very good information-gathering strategy. It's a way of controlling the conversation without having to do anything.

'Teachers are taught the "think time" rule, in which they are encouraged to wait longer than the usual 1 second for a response from students. By allowing 3 seconds, they are able to get a far greater quality of response in children they had previously thought of as slow and, therefore, stupid. It turns out that [these children are] thoughtful and have interesting things to say.'

HOW TO MAKE NEW HABITS (AND STICK TO THEM)

Harder! Faster! Better! Stronger! Isn't it just exhausting? Do any of our gargantuan efforts to exercise more, eat more healthily, drink less alcohol and be more productive ever come to anything? More often than not, no. According to U.S. News 80 per cent of New Year's resolutions fail by the second week of February.

That's because while there are lots of lovely short-term rewards to be had from 'being bad', there are few for being good. It's nice to eat crap (in the short term), whereas it's hard to go for a run, even though we know it will be good for us in the long term. The disappointment we feel from reneging on our resolutions means we are even less likely to attempt it again.

It is, unsurprisingly, difficult to create new, positive habits. However, with the help of behavioural psychology, it's not totally impossible.

DESIGN A SYSTEM FOR CHANGE

We need to design a way of reaching our goals which requires little or no willpower and effort on our part. Amazingly, such a system exists! Professor B. J. Fogg is the founder of the Persuasive Tech Lab at Stanford University, and he studies the ways in which companies like Twitter, Google, Instagram and Facebook purposefully design their apps and sites so that using them quickly becomes 'habitual'. He calls this field of expertise 'Captology' or CAPT (Computers As Persuasive Technologies).

When trying to cultivate new habits, he believes we need to 'design out' any need for willpower or motivation (both of which are a finite resource), and make it as easy and automatic as possible, and also to give ourselves constant rewards.

This insight is the foundation of his 'Tiny Habits' system of behaviour change.

THE THREE MUSKETEERS OF
HABITUAL BEHAVIOUR

Fogg's research has led him to believe that human behaviour runs according to systems. Rather than making it up as we go along, we have, over the years, devised habits and ways of doing things which become automatic.

According to Fogg, the three musketeers of habitual behaviour are:

Motivation

Why does your alarm clock go off in the morning? Because you want to get up and do stuff with your day. That's the motivation.

Trigger

The noise of the alarm is the trigger or instigator for the desired behaviour – getting out of bed.

Ability

Putting the alarm clock in a place where you'll hear it and be able to turn it off empowers your 'ability' to complete the task of waking up and getting out of bed.

When we're designing new regimes, we need to bear in mind: our motivation (why we're doing this), the trigger (what will increase our chances of actually doing it?) and our ability (how do we make it as easy as possible to do this?).

TINY HABITS, BIG CHANGES

1. Start small. Really, really small. No, smaller

Fogg believes that we should pick a task that is so small it's basically a bit of a joke. The reason being that small tasks require little to no effort or willpower, meaning you're more likely to actually complete the task. When it comes to habits, completion is everything. Completion means success, which in turn creates enjoyment and therefore motivation to carry on.

2. Find an anchor

An anchor is a routine that you already have, such as brushing your teeth, going to the bathroom or making coffee first thing in the morning. Anchor your new positive (ridiculously easy) habit on to the back of something you already do every day.

Complete this sentence:

After I (routine), I will (new behaviour)

For instance, Fogg, who works at home, decided to do two push-ups every time he went for a pee, which on average is seven times a day. What he found was then because doing two push-ups was ridiculously easy, he was able to up the ante to three, then four and so on. He now incorporates up to 100 push-ups into his daily routine.

3. Enjoy tiny thrills

According to Fogg, the human brain makes little distinction between meaningful successes and relatively small ones. The neurological reward we get from 100 likes on a Facebook post is the same as receiving a good book review from the *New York Times*. They're both just as satisfying. So doing things like looking in the mirror and saying, 'Yeah, well done!' after your two push-ups might seem silly but is actually crucial to building 'success momentum'. Athletes are constantly celebrating success, no matter how small the achievement. These 'tiny thrills' compound over time to create habitual and automatic behaviour.

HOW TO FOCUS

PAY ATTENTION. NOW, PLEASE! Because of the pings, beeps and melodious digital refrains which vie for our attention every day, Microsoft has discovered that the average attention span lasts just 8 seconds, which is less than that of a goldfish. Gloria Mark, who studies digital distraction at the University of California, Irvine, found that a typical office worker gets only 11 minutes between each interruption, while it takes an average of 25 minutes to return to the original task after an interruption.

The internet and modern telecommunications is bad for our brains, specifically, the bits of our brain that we use to focus on meaningful tasks, like writing a book, for instance. In *The Shallows: How the Internet is Changing the Way We Think, Read and Remember*, Nicholas Carr shows how the focused 'linear mind' has shifted to one which processes information in 'short, disjointed, often overlapping bursts – the faster, the better.'

But worry not. According to Daniel Goleman, author of *Focus*, we should think of our attention spans as muscles which can be

developed and made stronger via the cultivation of good habits and exercise. Deep focus means you can get the important stuff done more efficiently before you're interuppted by trivial distractions: Tindering, WhatsApping, Instagramming and laughing at lolcats.

Deep focus is also the 21st century's new superpower. While everyone else is blethering on Facebook about the new episode of *Game of Thrones*, you're in deep flow, maybe even writing the next *Game of Thrones*, or just getting your presentation ready for tomorrow's meeting that little bit quicker. Either way, here's how to increase your focus.

TURN IT OFF

Tucked away in the back cover of her book *NW*, writer Zadie Smith acknowledges 'Freedom' and 'SelfControl' for 'creating the time'. It turns out that 'Freedom' and 'SelfControl' are downloadable apps which block access to the internet. Jonathan Franzen went a step further by blindfolding himself and wearing earplugs while writing portions of *The Corrections*. Freedom was created by Fred Stutzman, visiting professor at the University of North Carolina, and is also used by Nick Hornby, Dave Eggers and Naomi Klein. Will Self types his first drafts out on a typewriter or uses pen and paper. For tasks which require deep focus, such as writing, turn off your devices, message alerts and, if possible, the internet. A delay of just 2.8 seconds doubles the chances of mistakes being made, according to a 2015 study published in the *Journal of Experimental Psychology*.

CHOOSE YOUR TIME OF DAY

There is yet to be any real consensus on the best time of the day to focus deeply, and psychologists believe that it depends on each individual's ultradian rhythm, the body's rest/activity cycle. Each person will feel in their body and mind the times of the day when they're able to concentrate most.

Participants in willpower and focus tests reveal that both are a finite resource. So for many, our brains may be at their most powerful 2.5–3 hours after waking up, before we have gone through a day's worth of bother and stress. Studies have also shown that the prefrontal cortex, the area of the brain most associated with creative thought, is at its most active during sleep and just after waking.

WORK IN SHORT, INTENSE BURSTS

Your brain can only focus intensely and do it's very best work for periods of 90–120 minutes. This is due to the ultradian rhythm, a cycle of brain activity which determines when we'll be at our most alert and high functioning. A study conducted by K. Anders Ericsson, a professor of psychology at Florida State University, of the schedules kept by prodigious violinists found that they typically practised in the morning for three sessions consisting of 90 minutes each, with a 20-minute break in between each session. The same pattern of focus and rest was discerned in the routines of other top performers, allowing them to get into what psychologist Mihaly Csikszentmihalyi dubbed 'flow state' – when the brain is working to its maximum potential.

CHOOSE YOUR ENVIRONMENT WISELY

The modern open-plan office with its constant distractions is not conducive to deep thought. According to Maria Konnikova writing in the *New Yorker*, these types of work spaces are 'damaging to the workers' attention spans, productivity, creative thinking, and satisfaction.' So try to find somewhere quiet if you work in one of these places or ask to work at home.

Temperature also affects focus. A 2004 study from Cornell University found that workers are most productive and make fewer errors in an environment that is somewhere between 20 and 25 degrees Celsius [68 and 77 degrees Fahrenheit]. Another from the Helsinki University of Technology in Finland says the optimum temperature is 21.6 degrees Celsius [71 degrees Fahrenheit].

MEDITATE

According to a University of California study conducted in March 2013, undergraduate students scored higher on memory tests and exercises requiring attention when they practised mindfulness and meditation for 10–20 minutes, four times a week, compared with students who changed their diet to a healthier one as a way to boost focus.

HOW TO NETWORK

Networking, as Julia Hobsbawm explains in her book *Fully Connected*, isn't just for work, although it is extremely useful for that; it's also for life. All of human life flows through networks of people and connections, for good and bad. Terrorism, gangsterism and fake news are facilitated by clandestine networks both real and virtual, but so are positive phenomena like breakthroughs in science, medicine and philosophy.

So how we network, whom we choose to connect with and the means by which we do it are hugely important. And in many cases, these choices can, quite literally, be a matter of life and death. A breakdown in communication between the distant bureaucracy of the World Health Organization and the on-the-ground agility of Médecins Sans Frontières helped to spread the deadly Ebola virus in Sierra Leone. Fake news is a symptom of networks gone awry, a breakdown in communication that spreads malicious lies.

'In the same way
that most of us now
know the difference
between a carb and
a protein, we need
a new literacy in our
understanding of social
networks, both real and
virtual, and of when
to connect and when
to disconnect.'

Right now, Hobsbawm argues, we are living in an age of information and network overload – or 'infobesity' – which is making us unhealthy. 'There is a stress epidemic in this country [in the UK] caused by too much information and connectivity,' says Hobsbawm. 'More than ten million workdays in the UK are lost due to stress, and yet our GDP is stagnant.

'In the same way that most of us now know the difference between a carb and a protein, we need a new literacy in our understanding of social networks, both real and virtual, and of when to connect and when to disconnect.'

Here are some of Hobsbawm's top tips for healthy networking.

GET FACE TO FACE

'Get off Facebook and get face to face. Reconnect with someone you know but take for granted. Organise and see ten people over the next ten weeks. At the very least phone someone you haven't spoken to in a while. Rekindle dormant ties. Keep in motion and progress your relationships rather than let them lie inert on the tracks of an electronic network.'

TREAT YOUR CALENDAR
LIKE YOUR BODY

'Be as meticulous about what you put in your diary as what you put into your body. Take back control of your diary; don't outsource it to someone else. There are only 168 hours in a week, and you spend at least a third of them sleeping. Your time is finite. Look at the patterns in your diary, look at what they mean to you and decide some patterns which work better. Choose specific times to clear out your inbox, and set aside a two- or three-day period in which to just think. This will help to cleanse your palate of the overstuffed commitments which cause stress, blockage and overload.'

IT'S NOT SALES

'Think "people base" not "database". Healthy networking is about spending time with people we know and trust and with whom we can build relationships, rather than some kind of transactional or fleeting vortex where it becomes a chore rather than a matter of taking care of yourself. Instead we need a more feminine way of conducting our lives. Feminine traits, such as emotional and intellectual intimacy and nosiness, come into their own.'

AVOID [STEREOTYPICAL] GROUPTHINK

'Surround yourself with people who think differently from you, who know different things, who are younger or come from a different background. Avoid "groupthink" and "hive mind". People think being at the centre of the action is essential, but I have found that this can disconnect from where the action really is, which is everywhere.'

HOW TO
OVERCOME FAILURE

You'd think, given the endless bragging that happens on social media, that everyone's career is an unending succession of successes, followed by a few triumphs, with the pièce de résistance served up before lunchtime.

This is nonsense of course – even a billionaire can have a bad day at the office. And when they do, they call up someone like Dr Tara Swart, a leadership coach who uses neuroscience and psychiatry to help CEOs in times of intense pressure, such as after a major failure or ahead of a challenge like a merger or IPO. Dr Swart, author of *Neuroscience for Leadership: Harnessing the Brain Gain Advantage,* calls the ability to deal with stress, 'resilience'.

'Resilience is not
only the ability
to bounce back
from adversity
but also the
strength to thrive
in situations
when confronted
with change and
uncertainty.'

'Resilience is not only the ability to bounce back from adversity but also the strength to thrive in situations when confronted with change and uncertainty,' says Dr Swart. 'I use neuroscience to help my clients to get back to good decision-making after a setback and to develop the cognitive resources necessary to achieve peak performance during times of intense pressure.'

When we suffer a major setback, Dr Swart says our appetite for risk diminishes as we become less confident. This can be a particular problem for people working in finance whose job it is to assess and take risks. 'Conversely, overconfidence leads to excessive risk and bad decisions,' she says. 'Our energy levels also diminish and with them our ability to motivate others, which is crucial when you are a leader.'

So here's what to do when you make a complete fool of yourself at work.

SHAKE IT OFF

Exercise is essential in our day-to-day lives, but is especially important when stressed, as it helps to increase testosterone and decrease cortisol, which is essential for getting back to peak performance. According to Dr Swart: 'Testosterone impacts on confidence and the appetite for risk.' She says that in extreme cases, some of her clients are prescribed testosterone supplements, but in general weight training will help boost testosterone levels. And for those who enjoy a protein shake, there's a chemical found in cabbage you can whizz up in your smoothie to give you a boost too.

'Cortisol is produced by the adrenal glands and is caused by stress and disrupts the sleep/work cycle,' explains Dr Swart. 'Physical exercise, in addition to boosting testosterone, has the beneficial effect of releasing endorphins and also helps to secrete cortisol out of the body. Magnesium supplements help too.'

BE MINDFUL

According to Tim Ferriss' book, *Tools of Titans*, in which he explored the habits of self-made billionaires, tycoons and corporate high-fliers, 80 per cent of the subjects studied practised mindfulness, which is something that Dr Swart strongly recommends. 'The main reason is that we need to articulate our emotions,' she says. 'Bottling up emotions such as shame, anger, fear, disgust, and sadness is dangerous. Even just writing your feelings down helps to decrease cortisol.'

REMEMBER THAT TIME
YOU WERE AWESOME

'You need to own your past successes,' says Dr Swart. Remember and visualise past successes to boost your confidence for a difficult task. 'Thinking about other people's successes will also help them seem more achievable. Try to think: "If another person successfully launched the IPO, then it must be possible."' Past precedents render challenges less threatening to the brain.

SAY IT NOW: I'M THE BEST
(NO, REALLY)

'Positive self-talk is proven to boost confidence. Having a series of positive statements either written down or in your mind can reprogram the brain's neural pathways and prevent negative thought patterns,' says Dr Swart. Even simple ones like, 'I am capable' or 'I make great decisions' can help to boost performance.

CHAPTER TWO

REST

WHY A LITTLE BIT OF ME-TIME IS GOOD FOR YOU

As Whitney Houston once sang, the greatest love of all is self-love. And what better way to enjoy one's marvellous self than on one's own? However, in our touchy feely, oversharey, inter-connected world, indulging in a little bit of me-time is considered quite deviant.

A 2014 study at the University of Virginia discovered that participants would rather subject themselves to an electric shock than be alone with their thoughts. Prisons punish the naughtiest offenders with solitary confinement. Sigmund Freud, who linked solitude with anxiety, observed that 'in children the first phobias relating to situations are those of darkness and solitude.' The UK government speaks of a 'loneliness epidemic' which for sufferers is as bad for their health as smoking ten cigarettes per day.

'In our touchy
feely, oversharey,
inter-connected
world, indulging
in a little bit
of me-time is
considered quite
deviant.'

So why then is being on your own so enjoyable?

First, solitude is different from loneliness. Loneliness is solitude gone wrong. Or an adverse emotional reaction to being on your own. According to Michael Harris, author of *Solitude: In Pursuit of a Singular Life in a Crowded World*, 'Solitude is a productive and contented time spent alone.'

THE 'FOUR IFS' OF SOLITUDE

Targeted, deliberate solitude is known by psychologists and neuroscientists to have wide-ranging benefits for the mind. Kenneth Rubin, a developmental psychologist at the University of Maryland, says that solitude is only considered beneficial on the condition of four 'ifs':

- *If* it is voluntary

- *If* one can regulate one's emotions effectively

- *If* one can join a social group when desired

- *If* one can maintain positive relationships outside of it

After all, no one is advocating that you become Mr Billy No-mates or relocate to a desert island for years of self-inflicted *Castaway*-style torture.

QUIT SOCIAL SNACKING

Sherry Turkle, author of the book *Alone Together*, says that we need to build in regular periods of solitude and abstain from 'social snacking' like checking Facebook, Twitter, email and Instagram, and also, build safe spaces away from the internet where we can enjoy quiet time. In her TED Talk, 'Connected, but alone?', she says:

'When we don't have the capacity for solitude, we turn to other people in order to feel less anxious or in order to feel alive. When this happens, we're not able to appreciate who they are. It's as though we're using them as spare parts to support our fragile sense of self.'

'Paradoxically,
solitude
helps us
appreciate
the company
of others.'

THE THREE BENEFITS OF SOLITUDE

Michael Harris believes that there are three main benefits
of solitude:

1. The ability to come up with new ideas

You can't crowdsource creativity. It does not happen during
brainstorms or with groups of people shuffling Post-it notes around
a wall. True creativity, the kind that mints beautiful new phrases
and comes up with original and interesting ways to solve problems,
a.k.a. Eureka! moments, is arrived at through the brain's default
mode networks (DMN), a complex series of pathways in our brains
which light up when we're seemingly doing 'nothing' on our own,
like when out on a walk or staring out of a window. Even looking at
a blank sheet of paper is enough to set off our DMN.

2. Knowledge of self

When we're with others, we're more likely to go along with what
the group wants and likes. Extended periods alone allow you to see
who you are outside of a social context. At the very least you'll be
forced to check out a new movie, piece of music, art, theatre, food
etc on your own, without having to rely on a computer algorithm or
groupthink. Who knows what you might find?

3. Absence makes the heart grow fonder

Paradoxically, solitude helps us appreciate the company of others. When you spend time alone, you're likely to think about the people you want to spend more time with, and make more of an effort when you do see them. Romantic relationships are often more intense, passionate and pleasurable after an extended period apart. Think about that the next time you fire off a bunch of emoji-laced texts to a long-distance lover. Why not try writing a letter instead? Delayed desire is more sexy and seductive.

HOW TO TURN OFF
(FOR A BIT)

Once upon a time, we dreamed of leaving the rat race to grow organic vegetables and make cheese in the countryside. Today, terribly nice, middle-class self-actualisers dream of one thing and one thing only: switching off our devices. We've never trusted them in the first place. They were for brash, self-important yuppie types. But then we got one of the damn things, and like everyone else we just could not stop.

The early data and research is not yet conclusive but some of it seems to confirm what we suspected all along: that there is a link between the rise in smartphone and social media use and the rise in mental illness, especially among teenagers. But link does not mean cause. Perhaps more illuminating is the fact that the Waldorf School of the Peninsula – where Silicon Valley execs send their kids to receive 'a renaissance education' – bans the use of smartphones and tablets.

Steve Jobs also did not allow his children to use touchscreens. Isn't this tantamount to tobacco executives quietly giving up smoking in the 1950s while publicly claiming there to be nothing wrong with it?

Whatever the reason, the idea of completely turning off is like the opening spread in a high-end Boden or J.Crew catalogue: a lovely middle-class dream which will never become reality. All of human life is mediated by technology now. There is no escape. But that won't stop us from trying. Oh no. Perhaps we'll become as sanctimonious, insufferable and holier than thou about technology as we are now about gourmet foodstuffs. Maybe there'll be some kind of organic, slow-tech movement. Until then, here are some realistic ideas for managing our tech addiction.

TRY AEROPLANE MODE

For those who work in digital media, perhaps as writers or content people, or social media strategists, or something equally tech-dependent, the idea of totally turning off is ridiculous. We need to be on for our livelihoods. And for Instagram. Amelia Diamond, writing in *Man Repeller*, hit upon the brilliant idea of making use of aeroplane mode on smartphones. You don't have to go through the rigmarole of turning your phone off totally, but instead, you can quickly flip on aeroplane mode during dinner, at a party, at the cinema or just before bedtime, as quickly and easily as you can turn it back on. Or there's something I call 'ghost mode' – which is to turn off vibrate and sound notifications.

Both give you power to deal with the incoming messages and notifications on your own terms, without having to pander to every little beep and ping as it comes in. Ahh bliss.

GET A DUMBPHONE

This is the next level of digital addiction management and not for everyone, especially those of us who need to use maps all the time to get around town. But the essential idea is a sound one. You can even get a nice-looking designer dumbphone now, like the ones from Punkt., which have no internet or app capabilities. Or you could try uninstalling all your apps... but the temptation still remains to download them again. Another option is to have a dumbphone, and then keep a small tablet with you, like a side arm, for emergencies. Both will drastically cut down phone use.

KEEP THEM OUT OF THE BEDROOM

Your bedroom is for two things, neither of which, when done right, requires the use of a smartphone or laptop. Turning your bedroom into a casino/entertainment centre/shopping centre is unlikely to help you get a good night's sleep. The blue light emitted by devices tricks the brain into thinking it's still daytime. Either stop all use of devices at least 2 hours before trying to sleep or keep them outside of the bedroom.

MAKE BETTER CONNECTIONS

You'd be amazed at how interesting, funny and attractive people can be when you give them your full attention. It's not only incredibly cathartic and freeing to not be harried by endless beeps and pings, you will also become more popular and loved as a result of cutting down your phone use. That's because it's so flattering, charming, and seductive to give someone your full attention and to listen properly to what they have to say. It's what everyone wants most in life: to be heard and attended to; for someone to care. In doing so, you will stand out like a brilliant beacon in a black sea of phone bores. This will lead to more invites to dinners and parties, more dates and job opportunities, and, in turn, more sex, money and fun. Quitting your phone creates a virtuous feedback loop of social jackpots.

'Quitting your phone creates a virtuous feedback loop of social opportunities.'

HOW TO FIGHT
JET LAG

It doesn't matter whether you fly private or cattle class – jet lag is an equal opportunities destroyer of holidays, business trips and returns back to work.

'Jet lag happens when we disrupt the body's circadian rhythms – our internal clock, which tells us when to go to bed, when to wake, and when to eat,' says Dr Cristina Ruscitto, a former member of a long-haul cabin crew, who studied jet lag for her PhD at the University of Surrey.

While there's nothing that can totally eliminate the disorientating effects of jet lag, there are lots of things we can do to ease the body and mind's transition back to normality. 'We can send signals to our body to get it to adapt more swiftly by being mindful of when we expose ourselves to natural light and when we eat food.'

So here are Dr Ruscitto's top five tips for fighting jet lag:

HOW LONG IS YOUR TRIP?

'There's a difference between frequent travellers and occasional travellers. Decide whether you want full adaptation or partial adaptation. For example, if you're going on holiday for two weeks, you want to have a nice time there, so therefore you're trying to adapt as much as possible; you don't want to be up all night. But for frequent travellers or for short stays, you will want to get back to your normal routine as quickly as possible, and so will not want to adapt to local time.'

SET REGULAR MEAL TIMES

'The circadian rhythm gets information from light and from meal times. It's a very simple approach: just eat in time with dark and light cycles – i.e. eat breakfast in the morning, lunch at midday, dinner in the early evening – even if you don't feel hungry. This is much easier than trying to stay awake. Our study of 60 cabin crew members found that those who stuck to set mealtimes after long-haul flights performed better on vigilance tests and had reduced levels of jet lag by day two.'

USE NATURAL LIGHT TO
RESET YOUR BODY CLOCK

'Light is a big resetter of the body clock. Being exposed to natural light is great for adapting to local time because that is what is going

to shift your circadian rhythm. The more light you're exposed to the quicker the process. Conversely, you can use blue-light-blocking glasses if you don't want to adapt to local time, especially if it's just a short business trip. These glasses were originally designed to help people fall asleep after using computer devices at night, but they are also good for manipulating the body clock if you're in a different time zone.'

GET A HEALTHY SLEEP ROUTINE

'Make your bedroom cool and dark. Try not to have caffeine before you go to bed, and try not to eat for at least an hour before you go to bed. It sounds simple, but lots of people don't have a good bedtime routine.'

TAKE NAPS

Contrary to popular belief, you don't have to struggle on into the night if you feel sleepy in a different time zone: 'Naps of 30 minutes are great. If you're trying to delay your sleep time but you're really struggling, you can have a short nap of 30 minutes to help you stay up longer.'

'Make your bedroom
cool and dark.
Try not to have
caffeine before you
go to bed, and try
not to eat for at least
an hour before you
go to bed. It sounds
simple, but lots of people
don't have a good
bedtime routine.'

HOW TO MASTER
THE ART OF
'ACTIVE REST'

'All work and no play made Jack a dull boy,' goes the proverb, but did you know that it's also likely his work is dull and uninteresting too? In *Rest: Why You Get More Done When You Work Less*, technology forecaster and Silicon Valley consultant Alex Soojung-Kim Pang debunks the notion that producing our best work requires relentless slog and miserable grind. Rest, he argues, is not only enjoyable in and of itself, but when done properly – something which he calls 'active rest' – actually increases productivity and is vital to creativity.

In fact, he says, many of the greatest minds of the past and present were intimately acquainted with the art of 'active rest' – comprising deliberate forms of relaxation and play that not only stop the mind and body from burning out but actively enhance and recharge the areas and networks of the brain responsible for deep analytical thought, memory and creativity.

'Active rest'
— actually
increases
productivity
and is vital
to creativity.

YOUR BRAIN IS WORKING
WHILE IT'S RESTING

Ever wonder why, when grappling with a difficult problem, the solution seems to pop up, almost like magic, just after a walk or some other kind of relaxing activity? As previously mentioned, default mode networks (DMN) are a series of connections in the brain that gently whir into action when it's seemingly at rest, offering up new ideas and insights ready to be accessed when the mind turns back consciously to the task at hand.

YES, JUST 4.5 HOURS OF
WORK A DAY IS ENOUGH

A quick look at Charles Darwin's daily routine showed that he typically 'worked' for just three 90-minute periods each day, with the rest largely spent on leisurely walks, letter-writing and time with his family. Not bad for someone who wrote 25 books, including *On the Origin of Species*, thereby revolutionising our understanding of nature and humanity. After analysing the schedules of some of history's most prolific and accomplished scientists, mathematicians and writers, Pang concludes that the optimum amount of time to work per day is just 4–5 hours, and no more than 20–25 hours per week. All of which builds the case for the idea that naps, exercise, holidays and walks aren't just nice-to-have optional extras in the quest to doing your very best work, but that they are actually essential to it.

TAKE A WALK, SOLVE A PROBLEM

Unfortunately, getting turnt up in the club doesn't constitute the kind of rest which allows you to do your best thinking and work (if only). Rest and exercise it seems is what gets the DMN firing. Experiments conducted by Stanford scientists Dr Daniel Schwartz and Dr Marily Oppezzo showed that subjects consistently performed better on tests that measure creative and lateral thinking while walking. Walking, it seems, allows the unconscious mind to do its thing, letting new ideas bubble up ready to be used when we're sat down and ready to focus consciously on a specific task or problem.

Likewise, the neuroscientist Sara Mednick discovered an hour-long nap – enough to allow for one dream – improves performance on memory and perceptual tasks.

HOW TO SLEEP
(PROPERLY)

According to Harriet Griffey in her book *I Want to Sleep*, a good night's rest is proven to help us concentrate more, maintain a healthy body weight, reduce stress, improve mood and improve athletic performance and coordination. While we know instinctively that sleep is good for us, barely a week goes by without some sociopath CEO or politician claiming to have addressed all their emails by four a.m. before starting work at 6 a.m. These people are weirdos not role models. You need your sleep.

But this attitude is slowly changing. In 2016, none other than the RAND Corporation worked out the business loss of poor sleep in the United States at $411 billion – a gross domestic product loss of 2.28 per cent. Even Arianna Huffington now writes books about

sleep and relaxation. Sleep is becoming a status symbol, and now technology companies offer designer 'sleep solution systems' – complete with all sorts of lights, gizmos and pseudo-neurological and scientific guarantees to ensure a better night's sleep for your upwardly mobile knowledge worker. Surely we don't want to commodify another vital human need, do we? Don't count on it. Silicon Valley entrepreneurs believe that in 2012 the sleep market was worth a cool $32 billion.

For the rest of us, in the trade-off between work, fun and sleep, it's always the last that gets cut back. Figures from the University of Hertfordshire show that six in ten adults in Britain are sleep deprived, which means getting 7 hours or less of sleep each night. That's 28 million people who are really knackered. Here's how to integrate a bit more shut-eye into your routine.

USE YOUR BEDROOM
FOR ONLY TWO THINGS

While *Mindhunter* is undeniably exciting, the action is best enjoyed from your sofa and not your bed. The blue light emitted from our devices tricks the brain into thinking that it's still daytime, making it harder to fall asleep properly. Devices should be kept outside of your bedroom. If all else fails, invest in a pair of glasses to wear in bed, which block the light emitted from electronic screens, and get yourself an alarm clock.

KNOW YOUR CHRONOTYPE

There are online tests available to discover whether you're a PMer or an AMer. While it's not much use if you have to work 9–5 and beyond, the information is useful for offsetting the quirks of your typology. For instance, AMers should aim to get all the important stuff done during the morning before the inevitable afternoon crash, and PMers should avoid lie-ins at the weekend, so as not to exacerbate their propensity to stay up late during the week.

INVEST IN YOUR BED

Like Goldilocks and her porridge, beds are a matter of trial and error, and personal preference. So go to a store and try out various mattresses until you find the one that is just right for you. However, when it comes to bedding, go for the most expensive, all-natural cotton, linen, or even silk sheets, that you can afford. Some people need a cosy duvet for a good night's sleep, in which case go for a down-filled one, rather than something made out of polyester. In both cases, natural fibres regulate temperature and simply feel better against the skin, just as your best shirts always feel better than your low-quality ones. Think of your sheets as the shirts you wear at night, and whoever you share it with will appreciate the luxury.

LIGHTS OUT

Invest in light-blocking curtains or black-out blinds, and make sure all your devices are turned off, including any standby lights. Your bedroom should be extremely dark when you turn the light off as that is how the brain tells itself that it's time for bed. Some people wear eye masks to block out the light.

TEMPERATURE

Your room should neither be too warm nor too cold, and there should also be plenty of air circulating in there. Anything lower than 12 degrees Celsius [53 degrees Fahrenheit] has been proven to result in bad dreams, and anything above 24 degrees Celsius [75 degrees Fahrenheit] is simply too hot for an undisturbed night's sleep. The optimum temperature hovers around 18 degrees Celsius [64 degrees Fahrenheit].

GOOD HEALTH
EQUALS GOOD SLEEP

A good night's sleep is the byproduct of regular exercise and a balanced healthy diet. Around 20–30 minutes of cardiovascular exercise, two to three times per week, will have a noticeable impact on the quality of your sleep. Likewise, your main evening meal should not be within three hours of bedtime, but do not go to bed on an empty stomach either.

AVOID CIGARETTES,
ALCOHOL AND CAFFEINE

Avoid cigarettes and coffee in the run-up to bedtime as both stimulate the central nervous system. Alcohol is a depressant, but while it might knock you out, withdrawal symptoms as it wears off during the night might affect your sleep. It will also make you want to go to the toilet and will dehydrate you, both of which can cause you to wake up.

HOW TO IMPROVE
YOUR MEMORY DURING
DOWN TIME

It is one of the quirks of the information age that while our phones can send us a notification to remind us we have a meeting with Dave at 11 a.m., we may well not remember who Dave is unless we go into our inbox or Google his name to find out. The constant bombardment of digital stimuli, combined with the fact that we rely so much on our devices to source and store information for us, means that our memories are shot. Birthdays, passwords, names – even really important ones – whizz through one ear and out the other. An academic study into the 'Google effect' showed that people today tend not to bother learning anything. Instead they remember where they can find it on the internet.

While this is progress of sorts – after all, what's the point in remembering all those facts if they can be summoned at the touch of a button – this increasing lack of memory is playing havoc with our social lives. We've all been there when disputes over film trivia among friends has to be settled with a quick Google, thereby disrupting the natural flow of conversation. Or when enthusiastically

telling a friend about a great new shop or restaurant, only for them to say, 'Can you text it to me?' – lest their scattershot brain not remember it without yet another beep and ping.

Memory, let's not forget, is one of the key signifiers of intelligence. There was a time when it was not uncommon for an erudite and charming person to be able to recite lines of poetry or passages of literature both to the delight of friends over the dinner table and as a means with which to fuel conversation. Sabinus, the Roman politician and soldier, had slaves who could recite whole passages of Homer to his dinner guests, who marvelled at the mental prowess of these human search engines. Quoting it from an iPhone is rather less impressive.

You'll also need your memory for when you're making a presentation during, say, a pitch, unless you want to ruin your chances by reading it out loud verbatim. Being able to memorise your arguments projects confidence and belief in your ideas – vital in any act of persuasion. Plato considered the ability to memorise speeches such an essential skill for oration that he included memory in his five canons of rhetoric. Whipping out your mobile is still, thankfully, pretty weird in a job interview, but not unimaginable.

Shared memory is also how we bond with one another, creating the social capital which creates funny in-jokes that are the basis for camaraderie and friendship. You can't google an in-joke or rely on an app to help remember it for you. So before yet another vital human function is outsourced to Silicon Valley, here are a few tips for improving your memory.

TAKE NOTES BY HAND

Research conducted by Pam Mueller and Daniel Oppenheimer, titled 'The Pen Is Mightier Than the Keyboard: Advantages of Longhand Over Laptop Note Taking', discovered that while students who took notes on their laptop were able to take down more of what their lecturers were saying, those who used pen and paper had a stronger conceptual understanding of the lecture and were better able to apply and integrate the material into other assignments. The very things that make laptops better for taking notes, namely speed and convenience, make using them a less efficient way in which to learn. Because note taking by hand is cumbersome and slow, it requires students to listen more intently and summarise the key points being made, distilling the essence of what was said. It is this real-time editing process or 'mental heavy lifting' which helps retention and comprehension.

TRY MEDITATION

Meditation can help to improve our 'working memory' – which is like the brain's notepad, a place where information is held temporarily. Researchers at the University of California, Santa Barbara discovered that working memory improved in students who practiced mindfulness and meditation, compared to a nutrition-based group. Mindfulness was also shown to improve standardized test scores and working memory after just 10 minutes of daily practice over two weeks.

GET MORE SLEEP

According to research by MIT molecular and developmental neurobiologist, Moheb Costandi, sleep is when we consolidate memories, and it is crucial to the retention and comprehension of new facts. Sleep deprivation can affect our ability to commit new facts to memory, and even a short nap can affect memory recall.

EXERCISE REGULARLY

A study conducted by the University of British Columbia found that regular aerobic exercise – walking, swimming, running etc – appears to boost the size of the hippocampus, the part of the brain responsible for verbal memory and learning. Weight training did not have the same results. Exercise is also proven to help us sleep better, which, as we know, is beneficial to memory.

CHAPTER THREE

SOCIAL

HOW TO BE CHARMING

While charm is easy to detect and hard to define, its principal benefit is pretty straightforward to understand. Charm, said Albert Camus, 'is a way of getting the answer "yes", without having asked any clear question.'

Note how in almost every Cary Grant comedy, it is the female lead, who, in the parlance of British reality dating show *Love Island*, 'sticks it on him' – not the other way round. It is Mae West's character, in *She Done Him Wrong*, who says, 'Why don't you come up sometime and see me?… Come on up. I'll tell your fortune.' And it is Audrey Hepburn, the only actor who could level peg with Grant in the charm stakes, who purrs gently in *Charade*, 'I don't bite, you know, unless it's called for.' Oh, go on then.

'Charm is a way of getting the answer "yes", without having asked any clear question.'

That Grant was gorgeous is undeniable. That he was one of the best-dressed men that ever lived – an influence on Giorgio Armani and Ralph Lauren decades after he died – is also undeniable. But good looks and elegant dress alone do not a charming man make.

There was a knowing detachment and irony to Grant – the nudges, the winks, the double-takes, the asides and the raised eyebrows – but always served up with a generosity of spirit. When Grant plays the romantic comedian, the audience and the female lead are always in on the joke. We laugh with him while laughing at him. We laugh together at hypocrisy and vanity – both our own and everyone else's. Who else could say, at the height of his fame, 'Everyone wants to be Cary Grant. Even I want to be Cary Grant.' After all, no one can be that charming, can they?

Benedict Cumberbatch? Eddie Redmayne? Or even George Clooney? Actors today take themselves very seriously, darling. And that isn't very charming at all. We're suspicious of charm. We value qualities like authenticity and emotional honesty, and tell-it-like-it-is straightforwardness. Just when you thought the show was all about shagging, look at the emotional candidness of all the contestants on *Love Island* or *The Bachelor*. This Oprah-ification of popular culture is not conducive to charm, so there aren't many charmers in public life today – no young ones at any rate.

Victims of charm can sometimes feel as though they've been had. Charmers often have run-ins with the law, particularly the tax man. The suits, the decent address in a smart part of town, the restaurants – it all costs money, you know. Charm is both superficial

·CARY·GRANT·

and manipulative. Lay it on too thick and charm soon becomes smarm. A charm offensive is the use of soft power to get hard results. Money, adulation, sex, social prestige – charmers want it all. Or, rather, they want you to want to willingly give it to them. No, really, you mustn't. Oh, go on then.

Can megawatt charm be taught, acquired or developed? Or is it innate? There have been no scientific studies of charm; but there are lots of dodgy people on the internet offering to make you more charming in just three easy steps. They're usually American. So no, it can't be measured and condensed into a pat formula. But it is delicious. And deadly. Charm – enjoy it. But don't be charmed by it.

BE NICE TO EVERYONE

Whether bike courier or maître d', heiress or tycoon, treat everyone with the same generosity of spirit: polite and interested, but never intrusive. Stephen Bayley, author of *Charm*, writes: 'Assume you have secret knowledge that every single person you meet will soon become very rich.'

DRESS WELL

Oscar Wilde wrote in *The Picture of Dorian Gray*, 'It is only shallow people who do not judge by appearances.' The charming man needs only one chance to make a good impression, and that will usually be in clothes which are simple and timeless, regardless of the relative formality of the situation he finds himself in. For instance, he won't wear a tuxedo to a house party – that would be stupid. But he won't dress like a moron hipster either. While it may be foolish to care too much about fashion, it is even more foolish to completely disregard appearances. You will be judged, and to think otherwise is evidence of an inherently basic intellect.

CHARM NEEDS AN AUDIENCE

Charm does a lot of its best work at parties and dinners. It is a social weapon. So parties in this sense are work. Enjoyable work, but still an arena in which to advance your interests. But subtly, of course. A charmer never 'networks' or 'schmoozes', or that equally horrible phrase, 'presses the flesh'. Instead, he makes friends, and he does so by being interested in and amused by others.

'It is only
shallow
people
who do not
judge by
appearances.'

BE INTERESTED IN OTHERS

Former British Prime Minister Benjamin Disraeli once said: 'Talk to a man about himself and he will listen for hours.' Lady Randolph Churchill, Sir Winston Churchill's mother, once made this comparison between Benjamin Disraeli and his great rival William Gladstone: 'When I left the dining room after sitting next to Gladstone, I thought he was the cleverest man in England. But when I sat next to Disraeli, I left feeling that I was the cleverest woman.' Charm is the art of subtle and, this is important, indirect flattery. Obvious and direct flattery is not charm, but smarm.

BE A SOURCE OF PLEASURE

Charm is really just the ability to make others enjoy your company. Anyone who has ever enjoyed themselves at a party or whiled away an afternoon in a nice restaurant drinking wine with a new friend, has both been charmed and been a charmer. Therefore, lighthearted and fun is always more charming than serious and critical. Likewise, an energetic, but not overly animated presence, is more charming than one that is lethargic and downbeat. Elegance and style will always trump crass vulgarity, as everyone likes to associate themselves with that which is refined, elevated and cultured.

HOW TO BE CHARISMATIC

Winston Churchill had it, while his successor, Clement Attlee, did not. Donald Trump has lots of it, while Hillary Clinton, alas, does not. Rappers have it by the bucketload, whereas writers and poets less so.

Charisma, like charm, is a set of attractive personality traits which inspire devotion in others. However, unlike charm, it is neither subtle nor lighthearted. Charisma doesn't do knowing irony. It does tub-thumping speeches at huge rallies in front of devoted followers. It can usually be found in generals, religious leaders, rockstars, rappers and politicians. Charm invites you out to dinner; charisma makes people go to war. Charm works on a one-to-one basis; charisma seduces on a mass level.

'Charisma is charm's less charming, and more combustible cousin.'

Charisma is charm's less charming and more combustible cousin. You can't be charming without being a little bit charismatic, but you can be charismatic without being charming. Andy Warhol, for instance, was said to have had a handshake like a wet rag and was slightly ill- and anaemic-looking – not very charming by any stretch. But he was undoubtedly charismatic, and stalked the New York social scene surrounded by a retinue of incredibly beautiful and influential people.

Nor is charisma essential for success. You wouldn't be able to pick Clement Attlee out of a line up, yet it was he who built the modern welfare state. Bill Gates and Mark Zuckerberg are not very charismatic, but Elon Musk (who has less money) has lots of charisma. Hitler, Mussolini, Mao and Stalin were all said to be charismatic. Theirs is a brand of charisma that tips over into narcissism, which is defined by psychologists as a pattern of grandiosity, need for admiration and lack of empathy. Indeed, charisma can make mediocre or not very nice people seem very special indeed.

The desire for charisma is also spawning a burgeoning sector in business coaching, whereby ordinary executives pay lots of money to be taught how to be charismatic. It works, apparently. When researchers trained middle managers and MBA students for 30 to 90 hours in twelve 'charismatic leadership tactics', such as using metaphors and gestures, they found that these people were perceived to be more charasmatic post-training.

PUT ON A SHOW

Winston Churchill knew a thing or two about what the fashion industry calls accessorising. In one of the most famous photographs taken of him, Churchill stands proud and immense, with a Thompson M1928 machine gun resting in the crook of his arm, a Romeo y Julieta cigar clenched in between his teeth and a homburg hat perched rakishly on his head. Churchill understood that his political message of defiance against the odds could be amplified with a few well-chosen props. He knew, simply, that when it comes to charisma, style matters.

BELIEVE IN YOURSELF

But there's more to charisma than accessories. Charismatic people often come into their own during times of dramatic change and turmoil. Hence, Donald Trump, who was able to motivate his followers with an intense sense of moral conviction and purpose, summed up by the now infamous, 'Make America Great Again' slogan. Charismatic people don't have fans – they have fanatics.

KEEP THEM GUESSING

Charismatic leaders cultivate a sense of unpredictability and mystery. You never know quite what they're thinking, who they really are or what they're going to do next. They often have a set of contradictory personality traits. Andy Warhol craved the limelight and yet seemed painfully shy and diffident. Mao lived like an emperor and yet was a proud member of the proletariat (although you could say that

this was hypocrisy more than anything else). However, he was also totally unpredictable and ruthless.

HAVE SOMETHING TO SAY

They may not always be the most learned or clever, but charismatic people have a remarkable capacity for highly emotive language. Language which is memorable and gets the heart pumping is a key tool in the charismatic leader's armoury. This includes catchphrases, slogans, rhythmic repetitions, chants, metaphors, personal stories and anecdotes, vivid imagery, alliteration and biblical rhetoric.

STRIKE A POSE

Napoleon spent hours in front of the mirror trying to mimic the gaze of his favourite actor, François-Joseph Talma. Mussolini would roll his eyes whenever he felt challenged. Jay Z throws up the Roc sign and his followers do too. All of this is a way of commanding attention, making you seem larger than life. Or like a god, as some celebrities are wont to make you think.

SAY IT LOUD

Charismatic leaders also have a particular tone, timbre and rhythm to their speech which is unique. Obama's is perhaps one of the most pleasing: deep and reassuring, with the cadence and rhythm of a jazz score. A rapper's flow, the style by which he delivers his raps, is his meal ticket. Think of Snoop Dogg's mellifluous sing-songy delivery or the one-two punch of Busta Rhymes' staccato attack.

HOW NOT TO
BE A BORE

If charisma and charm are both means with which we can seduce or attract a person or group's devotion, then the following are traits which will repel or put people off you. Of course, while we like to think that we are terribly witty, frightfully nice and innately elegant, all of us have it in us to be the complete opposite, and, usually, it's down to insecurity, anxiety and laziness. Parties, after all, can be hard work. So watch out for it. This is how you lose friends and alienate people.

'The blabber-mouth bore has no internal voice which asks, "Am I boring you?"'

THE BLABBER-MOUTH BORE

The blabber-mouth bore has no internal voice which asks, 'Am I boring you?' His stories are long and meandering, and seemingly without end, full of superfluous detail and totally lacking in any action, drama or humour. He speaks only of himself, asks no questions and shows no interest in anyone else. Remember what Voltaire said: 'The secret of being boring is to say everything.' Another tip to avoid being boring when telling a story is to inject a bit of emotion and revelation. Were you angry, frightened, embarrassed or regretful when such-and-such happened? Or, even better, say less than is necessary, like Andy Warhol, who once confided to a friend: 'I learned that you actually have more power when you shut up.'

THE VULGAR BORE

The vulgar bore lacks any sense of style or elegance. He thinks it beneath him to care, as his personality, character and wealth are what count. But, as is so often the case, while he may be wealthy, he's usually of pretty low character too. As G. K. Chesterton once said, 'Style is the dress of thought', and the vulgarity of the vulgar bore is actually a form of selfishness and arrogance. You see it whenever dot-com entrepreneurs insist on wearing baseball caps inside smart restaurants: the 'I'm so rich, I don't have to bother' attitude. Style is as much for the people around you as it is for yourself. We dress up for ourselves but also to show respect for others.

THE TIGHTWAD BORE

Tightness is so very unattractive and is still surprisingly common, particularly among the wealthy. Most tightwads don't realise they have a problem and think that the crumbs they throw your way are signs of their generosity. Tightwaddishness reveals a lack of generosity in all aspects of a man's personality and behaviour: no tightwad has ever been good in bed, ever.

THE MORALISING BORE

We are, thankfully, less moralistic and judgmental than previous generations. But that doesn't mean the moraliser doesn't lurk at dinner parties, say, when a friend confides that they are conducting an affair. When Oscar Wilde says, 'I can resist everything except temptation,' he is also making the point that unless you give into temptation, then, well, you'll turn into a judgmental, holier-than-thou moraliser and, therefore, not much fun at all. In any case, the moraliser isn't moralising for your benefit or out of any concern for you. They're doing it to make themselves feel superior. They don't have the courage to give in to temptation and so therefore doesn't want you to either. It's just another form of selfishness.

THE TECHNOLOGICAL BORE

The technological bore isn't just someone who can't help taking out their phone every ten minutes in order to show you a video of some lolcats or to Google some bit of pointless trivia in order to settle some pointless dispute – although that is very annoying. The technological bore also has the incessant need to take photos of every moment, both big and small; not so that an event can be remembered for posterity but so that it can be shown off on social media. It is especially bad at a party when, you know, you might want to be a little indiscreet, without the social-media FBI following your every move. Smartphones should never be a replacement for talking. In fact, they disrupt the ebb and flow of conversation.

HOW TO BUY
THE PERFECT GIFT

There's a scene in the Christmas special of *The Office* (UK version) that demonstrates the incredibly seductive and romantic power of a perfectly judged gift. As the rest of the Wernham Hogg employees exchange jokey secret Santa presents, Tim has quietly given his love, Dawn – who knows harbours the dream of being a full-time illustrator – a set of oil paints with a handwritten note that reads: 'Never give up'. With tears running down her cheeks at the powerful symbolism of this gift, she finally ditches her uncaring fiancé (who had cruelly dismissed her dream), and runs into the arms of her true love.

Gift-giving for the rest of us, though, is often a fraught and distinctly unromantic business. In psychological terms, a 'critical incident' is the stress caused by a traumatic event. In a study titled 'The Psychology of Gift Exchange' by Dr Karen Pine, professor of psychology at the University of Hertfordshire, researchers investigated the gifting experiences of 700 men and women and asked people to give examples of 'critical incidents' in relation to giving presents. They found that these trauma-induced stresses were usually caused by a gift not being well received.

According to the findings, common reactions to bad presents included non-verbal cues, such as a forced smile or stuffing the item back into the wrapping paper and putting it out of sight. Verbal honesty, such as asking 'I hope you didn't pay too much for this' was also common. And, perhaps worst of all, the re-gifting of the unwanted present, which cropped up again and again in responses: 'One person even got the gift back a year later that they'd bought for a friend,' says Dr Pine.

So how do we get it right? Here are three key things to bear in mind when you're picking out presents: appropriateness, empathy and effort.

1. Appropriateness

'Always aim for an appropriate level of intimacy,' says Dr Pine. For instance, it would be inappropriate to give your PA underwear, or vice versa. Generally speaking, anything that adorns the body or is symbolic of romantic love is to be avoided for work colleagues and friends – this includes fragrances, jewellery, underwear and clothes. 'Be careful not to overstep relationship boundaries,' says Dr Pine. 'It would be inappropriate to give something very personal to your boss that you might give to your boyfriend or girlfriend.'

2. Empathy

Dr Pine says a positive gift should carry some shared meaning. It should show some understanding of the other person and their needs. 'You're signalling a connection in the relationship,' she says. 'You're saying, "I know something about you; I know that you enjoyed this; I know that you love that."' Think about Tim and Dawn: she had confided in him her dream of being an artist, and he'd listened. When we get it wrong, it's because the gift is empty of meaning, or it shows a lack of consideration for the other person and their taste.

3. Effort

We appreciate gifts that the other person has gone to some effort to buy, particularly in intimate relationships. It symbolises caring, that you've spent some time on it, and that you've been thinking about the other person. That's why you should never buy your partner a bunch of flowers from the garage. Instead, Dr Pine recommends that you find out the flowers they like or their favourite colours and scents, and then personally choose a bunch of flowers on that basis. Just buying an expensive bouquet won't cut it.

SCENARIOS

Co-workers and colleagues

'With workers and colleagues, it's best to play it safe,' says Dr Pine. 'Also, a gift is not the medium with which to air out office issues.' Avoid passive-aggressive presents, such as a watch for someone that's always late or a book about organisation for the haphazard colleague. Something pleasurable, luxurious and neutral in terms of intimacy, such as a bottle of wine or box of nice chocolates will do.

Lovers and partners

According to UCL's professor of psychology Adrian Furnham, author of the article '*The Psychology of Christmas Gift Giving*' unattached men often view presents as 'fiscal foreplay'. Expensive gifts given early on in the relationship can be seen as sexual bribes, while cheaper presents later on in a relationship demonstrate complacency. According to Dr Pine: 'Early in a relationship, it can be a bit unclear whether you should buy a present or not. You should get something, but don't go over the top. The danger is you have to talk about where your relationship is going.'

Children

The temptation at Christmas is to give children everything they ask for, but Dr Pine says the festive season is also a chance to teach children to think of others: 'It's important to teach them Christmas isn't just about getting stuff. Involve them in making a picture for Granny, or baking her a cake, so they get involved. When adults buy all the gifts and kids are on the receiving end, they don't learn about the value of the exchange and about being considerate of other people.'

HOW TO MAKE
SMALL TALK

These days, small talk is seen by some as a big problem. Writing for *Wired* magazine in 2016, Dan Ariely, professor of psychology and behavioural economics at Duke University, and Kristen Berman, a behavioural consultant, declared small talk the 'lowest common denominator' of conversation and called for it to be banned from dinner parties. Instead, they believe we should fast forward straight to 'big talk': politics, religion and sex – even with complete strangers.

Unsurprisingly, British experts disagree. Catherine Blyth, author of *The Art Of Conversation*, describes small talk as: 'The overture to a conversation. Everyone is a portal to another world and small talk is the knock on the door.' Far from being meaningless, when done properly, light badinage often leads to meaningful exchange.

It is also enjoyable in and of itself, and far better, surely, when we might want to relax a bit, than to be accosted by an overly earnest stranger asking, 'So, what's your relationship with God?' halfway through a vol-au-vent?

What's more, research by networking experts, such as the founder of Editorial Intelligence, Julia Hobsbawm, has shown that job opportunities are more likely to be found via new acquaintances than among close friends. Rather than being inane and trivial, small talk makes your world bigger, opening it up to new possibilities, and in a far more interesting and unexpected way than, say, Google or Facebook might.

'People dislike small talk because of the pressure to perform. But you don't need to be Oscar Wilde,' says Blyth. 'It's important to remember, people hardly ever remember the content of what you say; they remember the feeling you left behind.'

Blyth's four steps for feel-good small talk are: 'Put others at ease; put yourself at ease; establish shared interest; actively pursue your own.' And with her expertise to hand, here's our guide to getting it right every time.

PREPARATION

Who's going to be at the party? Who would you like to meet? And, crucially, what do you want to talk about? What do you want to know? 'No one thinks it odd to wake up and think, "What do I want to eat today?" It's quite normal to prepare for a party by asking yourself, "What do I want to talk about today?" If you go in with no particular thing you're interested in talking about, immediately you're disadvantaging yourself,' says Blyth. In Georgian England, people noted down interesting things – bits of prose and poetry – in 'commonplace books' and referred to them for interesting conversational gambits. Mentally prepare and you'll reduce performance pressure.

THE APPROACH

Going to a party on your own is the social equivalent of parachuting in behind enemy lines in the dead of night, only far more dangerous. What if no one wants to talk to you? 'At a house party, hand round food and drink and you have a ready-made subject,' says Blyth. 'Or catch their eye, smile, then comment on something in the room: the decor, drinks, music, guests – but don't criticise.' Instead of trying to impress immediately with witty barbs and thus putting performance pressure on yourself, Blyth has a simple formula for keeping a conversation going. 'It's a bit pat, but it works: take two observations about where you are and then weave in something that's relevant to that person, and add a question to the end of it.'

(INDIRECT) FLATTERY GETS
YOU EVERYWHERE

'Some of the most unbelievably successful people I know are not the great intellects; they're not the great wits,' says Blyth. 'What they're extremely good at is making people feel wonderful in their company. They are interested and pay attention.' She cites Benjamin Disraeli, the great politician-cum-socialite, who befriended and charmed the notoriously taciturn Queen Victoria as one of the masters of small talk. Be careful with direct flattery, especially any comments regarding a person's physical appearance as this increases self-consciousness. Remember, the most flattering compliment of all is your full attention.

ASK FOR HELP

Other oblique forms of flattery, such as asking for advice and help, are also good. Blyth recommends finding a way to make others help you. 'Seek advice, seek help – people always love that,' she says. 'It makes them feel good. People are really helpful. The truth is, if you're talking to a stranger, they are a world of contacts and information and cultural reference points that you aren't part of. That's why I think small talk is amazing.'

BE NICE

'If you think you need to perform in order to engage people, you're looking at it the wrong way round,' says Blyth. 'What about the other person? There's always someone else that feels lonely, embarrassed and self-conscious. Find that person who's floating around. Everyone is prepared to engage someone with a smiling face and a listening ear.'

CHAPTER FOUR

LOVE

HOW TO BE SEXY

The writer Mark Simpson let loose the term 'metrosexual' sometime in the early 1990s, and men have never been the same since. Mr Metro is everywhere now, primping and preening himself, generally being quite tarty and flirty, and enjoying his new-found sex appeal. His younger, even tartier brother, the 'spornosexual', an amalgam of sport, porn and sex (named after his three main preoccupations in life), is epitomised by footballers such as Cristiano Ronaldo and reality TV stars in programmes like *Geordie Shore, Love Island, The Bachelor/Bachelorette, Jersey Shore* and *The Only Way is Essex*.

But not all men are enjoying the new freedoms afforded to them by the revolution of the past 25 or so years. Narcissus' pool of water has given male vanity a bad name. We have developed a zero-tolerance approach to vanity and affectation, while at the same time men

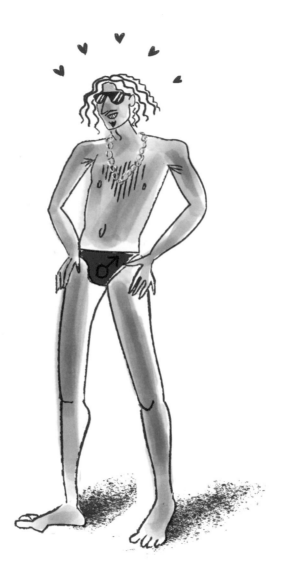

generally are more primped and preened than ever. Just look at how we sneer whenever an ageing male celebrity gets a makeover, or when we find out how much a male politician spends on his clothes and beauty regime.

But metrosexuality was never just about vanity and face masks. In his seminal essay, 'Here Come the Mirror Men', Simpson wrote: 'Contrary to what you've been told, metrosexuality isn't about flip-flops and facials, man-bags or manscara. Or about men becoming "girly" or "gay". It's about men becoming everything. To themselves. In much the way that women have been for some time.' It is then, the thinking man's response to feminism. The beginning of a new, more flexible definition of masculinity for a fast-changing world. So here then, are Mark Simpson's tips for being a better, sexier kind of man.

OBJECTIFY YOURSELF

The Guardian newspaper is brilliant in many ways. But it's got a problem with sex, desire and objectification, believes Mark Simpson: 'No one ever got laid by memorising a *Guardian* column. If you want to be wanted, you have to play the game. And the rules of the game are not up for discussion – just as sexiness itself can't be fudged. In a world of fake news and virtue-signalling, desire is the one thing we can actually believe in. The iris either dilates or it doesn't.'

'No one ever got laid by memorising a *Guardian* column. If you want to be wanted, you have to play the game. And the rules of the game are not up for discussion – just as sexiness itself can't be fudged. In a world of fake news and virtue-signalling, desire is the one thing we can actually believe in. The iris either dilates or it doesn't.'

SPEND MORE TIME
WITH GAY MEN

Spend less time with people who look and behave just like you, and you never know what might happen: 'Perhaps because they don't usually have a middle-class girlfriend/wife, gay men often have a no-nonsense – and no shame – approach to sex, along with the business of getting it. Even married ones. Especially married ones. They know all about male desirability, having basically invented it – and also a few things about how to dress up mutton as lamb.'

CHAT TO YOUR BUILDERS

You might have voted for Corbyn, but how many working-class people do you actually know or converse with on a regular basis? 'True, you may risk hearing political opinions that you don't agree with, but many builders, like gay men, don't go in for coy euphemisms,' says Simpson. 'They also know where to find all the best porn and the best gyms. In fact, if you can find some gay builders, you will score extra points.'

LET'S TALK ABOUT
MALE BEAUTY

Deliberately pander to the gaze of others. Look good for the people you fancy. There, he/she just looked at you. Now, isn't that delicious? 'Stop boring on about "grooming", "functionality" and "timeless style",' says Simpson. 'Who wants to be a bloodless, sexless euphemism? Start talking about whether something or someone is "hot" or not. Besides, not being afraid to – finally – bring the words "male" and "beauty" together in that still-verboten conjugation is pretty sexy in itself.'

DON'T FEAR YOUR BODY

The male body is not disgusting as you were told in school: 'You have a body. Yes, I'm sorry, it's true,' says Simpson. 'You are not just an incredibly expensively educated and eclectic brain that knows everything there is to know about coffee beans and craft ale. Bodies are necessary, not just as something to move that amazing brain around, and hang cool, tasteful, or sooo ironic clothes from, but also as something sensual and sexual to live in and advertise.'

ACCEPT THAT
'AUTHENTICITY' IS A FRAUD

That beard, that coffee, that stupid bike and the tasteful Scandi-blandi clothing will have to go. Not only is it not cool it's not very sexy either: 'Stop living in that adult day care called "Brooklyn" and come out and face the world in all its wonderful uncertainties and deceptions,' says Simpson. 'Fetishising "authenticity" as a style is a rather inauthentic way of living – especially if everyone else is doing it. It's a kind of avoidance strategy. Embrace affectation and artifice – and burn the plaid camouflage.'

HOW TO ARGUE
(POSITIVELY)

After you've read *Thank You for Arguing* by Jay Heinrichs, you'll never have another row with a partner, a relative, a friend or a colleague in quite the same way ever again. For Heinrichs, an argument is not a 'row' where one side shouts at the other, but an arena for smooth persuasion and canny negotiation, and one of the keys to harmony at home and in the workplace. Arguing positively takes the heat out of a situation and (seemingly) gives everyone what they want.

Heinrichs is an expert in 'rhetoric', the 3,000-year-old art of persuasion, invented by the Ancient Greeks. Whether it's a job interview, a politician's speech or a tricky question in a job interview, everything in life is a question of strategy, and the deft use of rhetoric

is the secret sauce behind the success of every persuasive appeal. It is the difference between war and peace, victory and defeat, or whether your opening line on Tinder leads to a date, sex and a lifetime of companionship, or is simply ignored.

It is the emailed pitch that resulted in the publication of the book you're reading. It is, in life, the difference between 'yes' and 'no' in situations big and small, and remains as relevant to technology workers in the ideas economy as it was to men in togas in Ancient Greece.

There are some who say that rhetoric is manipulative and therefore wrong and immoral. But in days gone by, we clubbed people over the head when they didn't give us what we wanted. Today, we use rhetoric to try and persuade them, which is surely much nicer and more civilised. We are all practising rhetoric, whether we know it or not, so why not do it more deliberately and skilfully?

SET YOUR GOALS

It is easy to confuse fighting with arguing. 'The basic difference between an argument and a fight: an argument, done well, gets people to do what you want. You fight to win; you argue to achieve agreement,' says Heinrichs. Point-scoring in an argument rarely leads to the prize of getting people to do what you want. 'My wife often says that I'm at my worst when I'm right,' he says. 'Our first instinct is to try and win on points. Do you want to prove yourself right? Or do you want someone to do something for you?' Remember, there are no prizes for being right, only for being persuasive.

'The basic difference between an argument and a fight: an argument, done well, gets people to do what you want. You fight to win; you argue to achieve agreement.'

KNOW YOUR AUDIENCE

'A boy who wants to use his parents' car to take a girl out on a date has a number of options,' says Heinrichs. 'But the most important thing to parents is safety. So if he says, "But, Dad, if I don't have the car I'm going to have go through a couple of bad neighbourhoods on mass transit, and we'll end up dead in a ditch somewhere," that's going to increase his chances of getting the car for the night.'

CONCEDE FIRST

An early tactical concession is often the quickest route to outfoxing the opponent and is a kind of rhetorical jiu-jitsu. A person pulled over by the police for speeding has roughly three options for a response. The first is to be sarcastic or belligerent to the officer. Another is to make up a spurious excuse for speeding – 'I have an emergency,' etc. The third is to concede that you were speeding, followed by, 'I must have been watching the road too closely. Can you suggest a way for me to follow my speedometer without getting distracted?' This third way appeals to his ego and takes the heat out of an argument, lets the officer feel superior, and may even get you off with just a warning.

USE THE FUTURE TENSE

Recriminations belong in the past. Using the future tense takes the anger out of a situation. 'My son had used all the toothpaste,' says Heinrichs. 'So I yelled, "George! Who used all the toothpaste?" and he replied, "That's not the point, is it, Dad? The point is how are we going to keep this from happening again?"' The most productive arguments use the future tense: the language of choices and decisions. Heinrichs follows this up with a quick tactical concession – 'Yes, George, you win. Now will you please get me some toothpaste?' After which George, feeling triumphant and therefore benevolent, duly gets his dad some toothpaste. Domestic bliss ensues.

ETHOS, PATHOS, LOGOS

Every argument is a blend of ethos, pathos and logos. Ethos is an appeal to character and makes others feel as though you share their values. Strategic admission of vulnerability can be used to make the audience identify with you. Logos is an appeal to logic. This is where tactical concessions and use of the future tense come into play. Pathos is an appeal to emotions and involves the use of humour and being sympathetic to the needs of your audience. Dial up or down any of the three, depending on who's listening. For instance, an audience of doctors may require more of a logos appeal, whereas R 'n' B singers and rap artists often use ethos.

HOW TO HAVE GOOD
BODY LANGUAGE

A lot of pseudoscience swirls around the observation and interpretation of body language. Sometimes it's as though an expert can reach into your soul just by looking at how you cross your legs. Most recently, we've had experts claim that the 'power pose', whereby you make yourself as big as possible by standing with your legs wide apart, actually increases the production of testosterone. Unsurprisingly, this theory was subsequently debunked.

Body language, like written language, is as much art as it is science. We know instinctively that man-spreading is inconsiderate and liable to make a man look quite insecure. Someone looking at a man with his legs spread wide apart on the train might think: 'What on earth is he trying to prove?' We can 'feel' when a smile is genuine, and can tell when someone isn't at their best when their shoulders are slumped.

One person, who 'feels' body language more than most is Les Child. A former dancer for the prestigious Michael Clark and Lindsay Kemp companies, he is now hired by fashion brands such as Gucci and Louis Vuitton to coach models in how to boost their stage presence and to get into character for shows and shoots. He's even been on tour with the Rolling Stones to teach Mick Jagger a few moves. So here then are his top tips for developing a more welcoming and friendly style of body language.

OPEN GESTURES

Open gestures help to communicate friendliness when talking to someone, says Child: 'Looking someone in the eye and smiling. Opening your arms and palms. Gesturing as though you're giving them something. Pointing your toes and hips toward the person you're talking to. All of these things demonstrate an open and interested countenance.'

'Looking someone in the eye and smiling. Opening your arms and palms. Gesturing as though you're giving them something. Pointing your toes and hips toward the person you're talking to. All of these things demonstrate an open and interested countenance.'

THE MIRROR IS YOUR FRIEND

Generally, especially in Britain, men are taught to not admire one's reflection too much, and to use mirrors only when absolutely necessary. But not so for Les Child: 'Life, going from A to B, is all performance. Try to look at yourself as objectively as you can, and imagine how another person will see you. Put your favourite music on and stand in front of the mirror and get to know yourself.'

He recommends having at least one full-length mirror and a smaller one just for the face. 'If you have the space, walk towards a full-length mirror. Practise a deliberate and confident walk. You can also use it to practise standing in different ways and, if required, to adjust and correct posture.'

Finally, try talking and practising presentations in front of the mirror, so as to experiment with different gesticulations, looks and expressions. 'There'll be points you want to emphasise. So you might do that with a hand gesture or a particular look. A mirror helps you to practise self-expression.'

DON'T OVERDO IT

Confident body language is a question of balance, and we tend to overcompensate when we're feeling insecure or threatened. Sit up straight but don't sit ramrod straight like a sergeant major. Smile, but not so much that you look like a loon. Give a firm handshake but don't crush fingers. 'Less is more,' says Child. 'Keep movements measured and deliberate. Not too much arm waving, not too much rolling of the eyes.' He recommends observing Cary Grant: 'He had a wonderful way of moving. Very elegant and masculine.'

ON A DATE

As someone who has worked with the world's top supermodels, Child knows more than most what people want on a date. 'First, women like an open, comfortable, interested countenance, and a relaxed disposition,' he says. 'So try not to show nerves by moving around too much or fidgeting. Lean in towards her to show that you're interested in what she has to say. And avoid crossing your arms and legs, especially if you are sat opposite one another, as this puts an unnecessary barrier between you. After that, it's about striking a balance between confidence and humility. So no power poses, but no hunched shoulders either. Ultimately, there are no pre-canned manoeuvres which will guarantee success. It's about observing and reacting accordingly. Her smile, the way she looks at you, the positioning of her body, all of these will tell you how she feels about you.'

HOW TO
MAKE FRIENDS

A 2015 study by the Movember Foundation, the charity behind the annual fundraising event in which men grow moustaches for the month of November, found that some 2.5 million men in the UK do not have a single friend they could turn to for help or advice in a crisis. The same study also discovered men's chances of friendlessness almost trebles between their early twenties and late middle age, with married men less likely than single men to say they have friends to turn to outside the home.

WHY ARE MEN SO LONELY?¹

Platonic friendships between men are often laughed at. Look how we commonly use the portmanteau 'bromance' to affectionately mock close friendships between men, or how in hip-hop culture open admiration for another man is sometimes appended with the phrase 'no homo'. Needing a friend implies weakness and vulnerability. Talking and sharing, the basis upon which friendships are formed, are seen as effeminate. Tenderness is often derided for being that little bit less than platonic.

All of which would be mildly amusing if it weren't set against the context of a 2015 study by the charity CALM (Campaign Against Living Miserably), which showed that four in ten men have thought about taking their own lives at some point. Clearly, friends are important, be they football friends, work friends, or just friend friends. Friendship, after all, is one of the basic human needs.

IT'S OK TO BE VULNERABLE
(NO ONE CARES)

'If you want some new friends, you're going to have to actively go out there to try and make some, and that makes you vulnerable, because you're saying, "I don't have all the friends I need,"' says Oliver Burkeman, columnist for *The Guardian* newspaper and author of *The Antidote: Happiness For People Who Can't Stand Positive Thinking*. 'The counterpoint to that is once you cross that border and let yourself be vulnerable, you often find that the harsh judgment you feared does not happen. Not because people are especially nice, but because they're so wrapped up in their own insecurities they simply don't have the time to think about yours.'

'Friendship occurs through a reciprocal admission of vulnerability,' says Burkeman. What makes other people like us are not qualities,such as intelligence or good looks, but our ability to share with them secrets that, if revealed, will result in our humiliation. Friendship flows from trust and acceptance.

Strategic admissions of vulnerability can also be very flattering. 'It's called the Benjamin Franklin effect,' says Burkeman, 'meaning that if you ask a favour of someone, like their advice on something important to you, it makes them feel like a trusted expert and a good person.'

BE HONEST

The old adage, 'To make a friend, be a friend' is more relevant than ever. 'Men like people who treat them honestly,' says Professor Geoffrey L. Greif of Maryland University's School of Social Work. 'They need to know that their friends have their back and will stick up for them when things aren't going well. They want their friends to be straight-talking and trustworthy. For instance, if I open up and tell you my secrets or reveal my weaknesses, I need to feel that you won't make fun of me.'

MAN-DATE

'Men tend to conduct their relationships shoulder to shoulder, whereas with women it's face to face,' says Greif, who is the author of a study titled 'Buddy System: Understanding Male Friendships', based on interviews with 400 men and 100 women and one of the largest studies of its kind to date. 'This means, in general, men go to the pub to watch the game or take part in some kind of sport. Women tend not to need a reason to meet up to increase friendship. They will meet up for coffee to just talk. Men tend to need an activity as a precursor to pursuing a friendship.'

Try taking a night class or joining a club in order to meet new people. Or, if you've met someone you like, rather than just asking if they want to hang out, you might feel more comfortable inviting them out for a round of golf or some other kind of activity that you think you'll both find fun. A shared activity helps to break the ice and create a shared history, which will hopefully lead to friendship.

IT'S NOT A COMPETITION

Who can pull the most birds? Who's got the funniest banter? Who's the cleverest? Men are socialised to compete with one another, which is fine, but that shouldn't be allowed to overshadow friendship. 'Competition isn't friendship, and it sometimes makes it difficult for men to reach out to one another,' says Greif. 'Try to get past it.'

'Competition isn't friendship, and it sometimes makes it difficult for men to reach out to one another. Try to get past it.'

EPILOGUE

This book will hopefully have encouraged you to cast a more discerning eye over some of the sillier ideas and trends which tell us how we should be and how we should live.

Though wide ranging in its tips and advice, there are some repeated themes:

Actual contact with an actual person will always be more useful and satisfying than contact which is mediated by a computer or smartphone.

An intelligent and motivated individual will always be better at coming up with good ideas and be more productive than groupthink in a brainstorm.

Sex and beauty will always be more fun than po-faced moralising.

You shouldn't try to outsource your brain to the internet.

And most important of all:

Wry and sceptical is often much 'nicer' and certainly more honest than the veneer of 'niceness' and 'authenticity' offered to us by therapy culture and social media likes and shares.

So here then, to conclude, is an essay by Peter York, co-author of the *Sloane Ranger Handbook* and author of *Authenticity is a Con*.

'Eclectic is a seriously
overused word now
but at its heart is
something of real
value, the idea
of making your
own choices from
different ideologies,
aesthetics or periods.'

HOW TO BE A NICER
TYPE OF PERSON

by Peter York

I don't want to be *judgemental* about consuming decisions. There's so much more to worry about – like the counter-gravitational survival of Donald Trump or the implications of Brexit for 99 per cent of ordinary Brits.

But then again I do. I want people to be properly sceptical and British about practically everything *except* Europe. I want them not to adopt fatuous airhead forms of words. I want them not to wear trainers for anything except sport. I want them not to hanker after cookie-cutter high-rise houses and flats which make home look just like work.

And I want them not to take up ideas that derive from American therapy culture. I want them to know that they may *not* be OK, that they may not be all that interesting until they've actually done something. And that self-branding is a cruel joke perpetrated by people like me on them – one that some of us have the grace to be sorry about now.

All this, I should say, isn't fogeyism; I want people to welcome the *real* modernity, the innovations that *really* change things, from iPads to remote medicine, I'm just warning them about 'shell modernism' – all those areas of modern life where a carapace of modernity is fitted over the unchanged old stuff like a porcelain veneer over a crooked yellow stump.

Real modernity – a substantive life-changing innovation – has benefits so self-evident that it doesn't need 'high design' to sell it. It's the other way round; it's when nothing is happening that life's window dressers and cosmetic dentists have to work frantically to give the impression of progress.

In the 1950s, when American cars were mechanically clunky, heavy and backwards, General Motors design king Harley Earl devised a constantly changing fashion show of brilliant carapaces; car designs full of metaphors of modernity, rocket fins to the back – this car could go to the moon! – and Hollywood smiles to the front. The moment real new technology appeared, and after we'd *really* gone to the moon, the magnificent shells shrank back to something more modest.

If I labour this point, it's to say don't build your personal pitch about something essentially commoditised – a ready-made identity based on something as one-dimensional as belonging to an age cohort – just being a millennial is meaningless, and even being a digital native isn't much better. *Work it out for yourself.*

Eclectic is a seriously overused word now, but at its heart is something of real value, the idea of making your own choices from different ideologies, aesthetics or periods.

And while we're thinking about words, never use any of the following with a straight face:

- authentic

- artisan

- creative

- passionate

- vibrant

or people *will* think you're an airhead.

AUTHOR
BIOGRAPHY

Alfred Tong is from London,
studied at the London College of Fashion
and writes for *GQ* and *Mr Porter.*

Other Books by Alfred Tong:

The Gentlemen's Handbook:
The Essential Guide to Being a Man

The Gentleman's Guide to Cocktails

ILLUSTRATOR BIOGRAPHY

Sarah Tanat-Jones is an illustrator based in London.
Her favourite things to draw are portraits,
food and architecture, and her favourite
museum is the British Museum.

She helped gather visual research for this,
her second full-length illustrated book,
by searching for images of Ralph Lauren
male catwalk models. It was a tough job,
but she got through it.

ACKNOWLEDGEMENTS

Seeing as I couldn't get on the phone to Castiglione, Machiavelli, and Wilde et al., I've done the next best thing. So many thanks to Peter York, Mark Simpson, Oliver Burkeman, Jocelyn K. Glei, Dr Tara Swart, Jay Heinrichs, Les Child, Catherine Blyth, Karen Pine and Julia Hobsbawm for taking the time to share your thoughts with me. And many thanks too to Alexia Inge, Pravin Muthiah, Adrian Holdsworth, Toby Hart, Cathy Giles, Gordon McCree, Ophelia Aasa, Percy Parker, James Robinson, Henry Rodrick, Simon Lewis (a.k.a. the Black Dragon), Omar Swanson, Phil Smiley, Nathan Miller, Max Woodhead, Lucy Clemence, Chantal Young, Lucy Hawkes, Richard Tong – and all my friends – for, quite simply, being interesting and funny at dinner, over drinks and at parties. It's conversation that makes books happen, not smartphones.

A version of the articles on pages 12, 20, 40, 44, 58, 66, 72, 116, 122, 136, 142, 150 were first published on MrPorter.com, The Daily. Many thanks to editor of The Daily, Adam Welch for commissioning.

The Thinking Man's
Guide To Life

First published in 2018 by Hardie Grant Books,
an imprint of Hardie Grant Publishing

Hardie Grant Books (London)
5th and 6th Floors
52–54 Southwark Street
London SE1 1UN

Hardie Grant Books (Melbourne)
Building 1, 658 Church Street
Richmond, Victoria 3121

hardiegrantbooks.com

British Library Cataloguing-in-Publication Data.
A catalogue record for this book is available from
the British Library.

ISBN: 978-1-78488-155-9

Publisher: Kate Pollard
Senior Editor: Molly Ahuja
Editorial Assistant: Eila Purvis
Cover and Internal Design: Stuart Hardie
Copy editor: Sarah Herman
Proofreader: Victoria Lyle
Indexer: Cathy Heath
Colour Reproduction by p2d
Printed and bound at Toppan Leefung, DongGuan City, China

A version of the articles on pages 12, 20, 40, 44,
58, 66, 72, 116, 122, 136, 142, 150 were first published
on MrPorter.com, The Daily